PUZZLE QUEST

The magician's library

Written & illustrated
by Kia Marie Hunt

Published by Collins
An imprint of HarperCollins Publishers
HarperCollins Publishers
Westerhill Road
Bishopbriggs
Glasgow G64 2QT

www.harpercollins.co.uk

HarperCollins Publishers
1st Floor, Watermarque Building
Ringsend Road
Dublin 4, Ireland

10 9 8 7 6 5 4 3 2 1

© HarperCollins Publishers 2022
Collins® is a registered trademark of HarperCollins Publishers Limited

ISBN 978-0-00-853212-3

Printed and bound in the UK using 100% renewable electricity
at CPI Group (UK) Ltd

Publisher: Michelle I'Anson
Author and Illustrator: Kia Marie Hunt
Project Manager: Sarah Woods
Designer: Kevin Robbins

PUZZLE QUEST

The magician's library

Written & illustrated
by Kia Marie Hunt

In a dusty corner of your local library, you find a strange, old and tattered book of stories.

When you open it... Whooosshh!

You are whisked away to the biggest and most colourful library you have ever seen! There in the centre, perched on a stack of books, is an owl with a cape and spectacles.

Okbo the owl is both a librarian and a magician, but their magic is a little rusty.

Okbo

The book you picked up was supposed to be a portal to all kinds of story worlds, but Okbo's spell to put it back together again went wrong and now the pages and stories are all mixed up!

Will you step into the enchanted book to help put the stories back together again?

Jump into the pages, explore each story and find all the missing characters. Be ready to solve more than 100 fun puzzles, collecting clues along the way!

Things you'll need:

* **This book**
* **A pen or pencil**
* **Your amazing brain**

That's it!

Will YOU take on the quest?

Psssst!
Always look out for
this quill symbol:

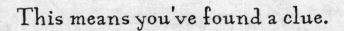

This means you've found a clue.

Write down all the clues you find in your Clue Logbooks (on pages **30, 54, 78, 102** and **126!**)

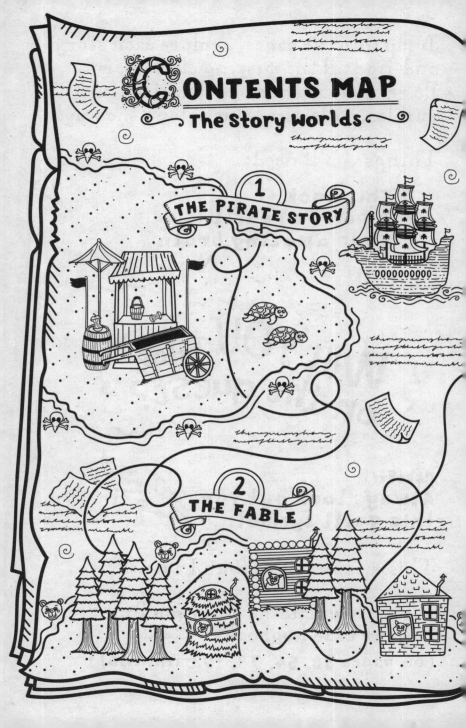

CONTENTS MAP
The Story Worlds

1 THE PIRATE STORY

2 THE FABLE

SHIVER ME TIMBERS!

As you step into the book's magic pages, the first tale you enter is one of pirates.

Prepare for a swashbucklin' adventure full of feathered fun, plank walkin' puzzles and hidden treasure tasks!

Remember to keep an eye out for this symbol: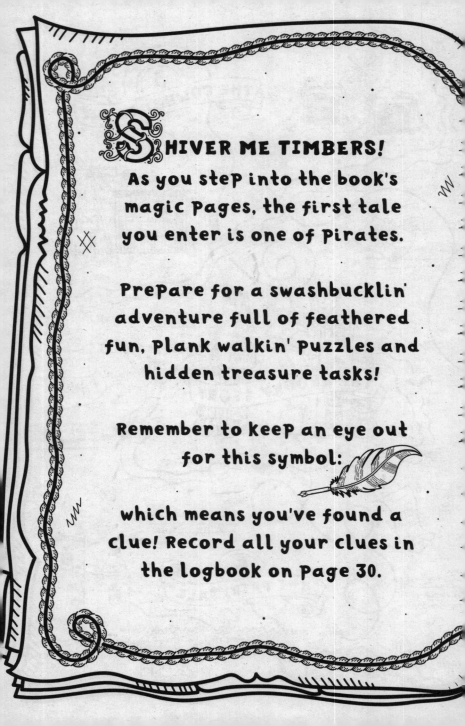

which means you've found a clue! Record all your clues in the logbook on Page 30.

THE PIRATE STORY

You find yourself on the outskirts of a seaside town called Squarrk. All you have in your pockets is a big ball of wool, a rolled-up palm leaf scroll and a few gold coins, how curious...

Follow the tangled paths. Which one will take you all the way into the town of Squarrk?
Write your answer into this box.

C

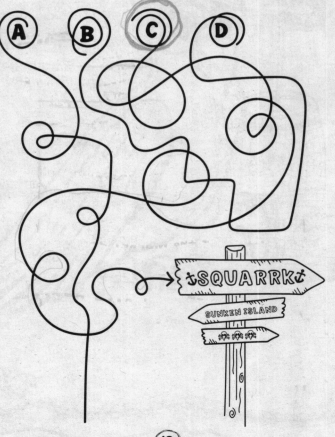

Squarrk is a very quiet town. You find a market that looks like it was bustling and busy once, but has recently been abandoned. What a mess!

Can you find and circle all the things from the list below in the picture of the market above?

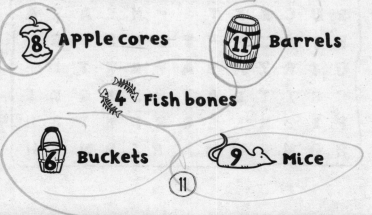

8 Apple cores

11 Barrels

4 Fish bones

6 Buckets

9 Mice

You're about to leave when you notice one small stall at the back of the market that isn't abandoned, it is full of fresh food! You go to explore...

Can you find all eight food items from the list in the wordsearch below? Words may be hidden in the grid horizontally or vertically.

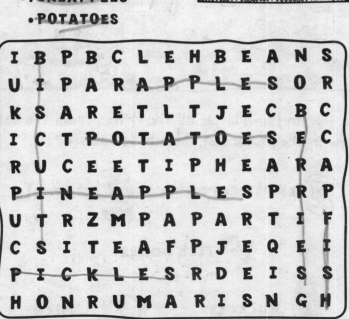

- APPLES • BEANS
- BERRIES • BISCUITS
- FISH • PICKLES
- PINEAPPLES
- POTATOES

```
I B P B C L E H B E A N S
U I P A R A P P L E S O R
K S A R E T L T J E C B C
I C T P O T A T O E S E C
R U C E E T I P H E A R A
P I N E A P P L E S P R P
U T R Z M P A P A R T I F
C S I T E A F P J E Q E I
P I C K L E S R D E I S S
H O N R U M A R I S N G H
```

Sitting behind the stall is a small, sad-looking otter – finally, another character to talk to!

Use the symbol Key to crack the code and fill in the gaps to reveal what the otter tells you...

A	D	E	F	G	H	I	L	M	N	O	P	R	S	T	Y

MY **SHIP** CAME IN **LATE**

AND I **MISSED** SQUARRK'S

FOOD **SHOPPING SEASON**.

NOW I HAVE **ALL** THIS

FRESH FOOD AND **NO ONE**

TO **SELL** IT TO. WOULD YOU

LIKE TO BUY **ANYTHING**?

(This symbol means this letter is your very first clue, congratulations! Don't forget to write it into your Clue Logbook on page 30!)

You feel bad for the otter so you use your coins to buy some food.

Now, you're in a pirate story, so you should probably head towards the sea, right? The otter tells you to follow the baby turtles if you want to get to the beach.

Make your way from start to finish.
You can move up, down or sideways, but you can't move diagonally and you must only follow the baby turtles with odd numbers.
The line has been started off for you.

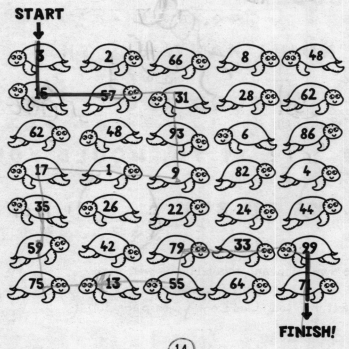

When you make it to the beach, you see a ship on the horizon coming closer and closer...

Which silhouette correctly matches the ship? Circle your answer...

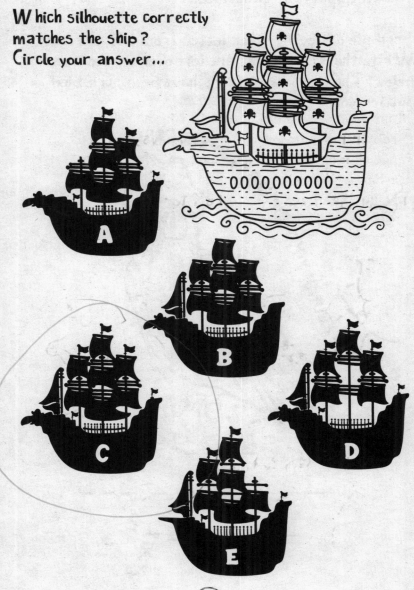

When the ship arrives, a parrot pirate called Captain Redbeak comes to greet you and to ask you an important question...

Scribble out every other letter from left to right. Write the letters that are left over on the lines below. The first two letters have been scribbled out for you.

A____!

___ ___ ___ ____ ____

____ ___?

Woah! It turns out the rolled-up leaf in your pocket isn't just any old leaf, it's a treasure map! You unravel it and hand it over to Captain Redbeak, who seems very happy with you.

Can you find and circle all six differences between these two pictures of the palm map?

You step foot on Captain Redbeak's huge pirate ship and take a look around. Are ye ready for an adventure, scallywag!?

Can you find all eight pirate ship words from the list on the opposite page in the wordsearch below? Words may be hidden horizontally or vertically.

```
I R P B C L E H B I J
U J P A R A N C H O R
K N A R E T L T J E C
I G T R W S W O R D C
R S C E E T I P H X A
U H H L D F T S Q M P
U I R Z M P A P A G T
C P D U M M E L T N A
O V E R B O A R D S I
H O N R U M A R I G N
O R U T H I U Y P E B
```

ANCHOR

BARREL

CAPTAIN

CREW

OVERBOARD

PATCH

SHIP

SWORD

The 19 crew members aboard this ship are all parrots! There used to be 20 of them until one went missing at sea just recently.

It's a bit strange that birds who can fly choose to spend all their time aboard a ship, but you don't fancy asking these fierce-looking pirates too many questions...

Instead, you try to imagine other kinds of birds as pirates and sailors.

3 letters
EMU

4 letters
HAWK

5 letters
EAGLE
STORK

6 letters
FALCON
PARROT
TOUCAN
TURKEY

7 letters
BUZZARD
OSTRICH

8 letters
FLAMINGO

9 letters
ALBATROSS

Place each of the bird words from the list on the opposite page into the empty squares to create a filled crossword grid. Each word is used once so cross it off the list as you place it to help you keep track.

You have nearly reached the treasure when you see what you think are shark fins swimming closer...

Uh oh! They are not shark fins, they are the ears of something even more dangerous!

Use the grid references to work out each letter and reveal the name of the creature. The first letter has already been done for you.

G
2✳ 3☠ 1◉ 4✳ 4◉   1⚓ 1◉ 4◉

1◉ 3✳ 2⚓ 3☠ 3◉

Solve the number problem below each letter in the Key. Then use the answers to fill in the gaps and find out what happens next. The first letter has already been done for you.

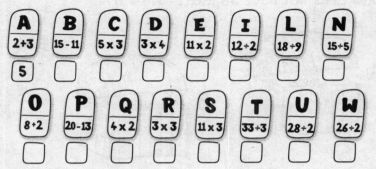

A	B	C	D	E	I	L	N
2+3	15-11	5 x 3	3 x 4	11 x 2	12÷2	18÷9	15÷5
5							

O	P	Q	R	S	T	U	W
8÷2	20-13	4 x 2	3 x 3	11 x 3	33÷3	28÷2	26÷2

THE G _ A _ _ _ A _ _ _ _ _ _ TRIES TO ATTACK
    6 5 3 11   15 5 11 33 8 14 6 12

THE PIRATE SHIP, BUT YOU USE YOUR

_ _ G _ A _ _ OF _ _ _ _ TO _ _ _ _ _ A _ _ IT.
4 6 4 5 2 2   13 10 10 2 12 6 33 11 9 5 15 11

_ A _ _ LOVE PLAYING WITH _ _ _ _ , BUT THIS
15 5 11 33   13 10 10 2

BIG _ _ _ _ _ 'S _ _ _ A _ _ _ _ GOT ALL
   33 8 14 6 12   11 22 3 11 5 15 2 22 33

_ A _ G _ _ _ UP, GIVING YOU AND THE
11 5 3 2 22 12

CREW ENOUGH TIME TO _ _ _ A _ _ !
                 22 33 15 5 7 22

Thanks to your quick thinking, you and the parrot pirate crew make it all the way to 'X marks the spot'. But instead of finding one treasure chest like you had all expected... you find SEVEN!

Odd one out: which of the treasure chests below does not have an identical twin?

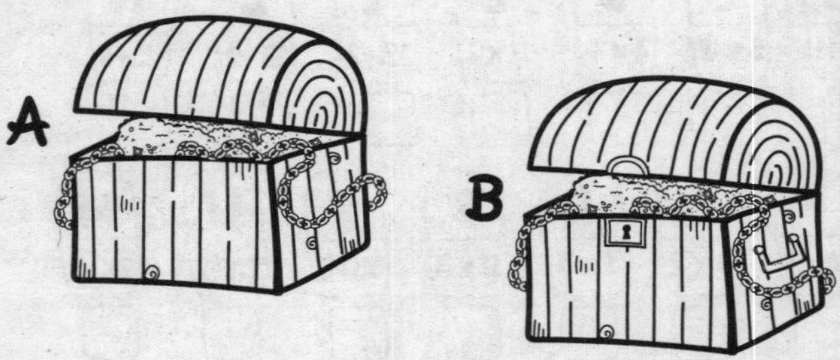

A

B

C

D

F

E

G

You don't get much of a chance to celebrate finding the treasure, because you can hear Captain Redbeak shouting something angrily from the ship...

Cross out any letter that appears more than once in the grid below. Write the letters that are left over on the lines below in the order they appear, and a hidden word will reveal itself. Letter I has been scribbled out to start you off.

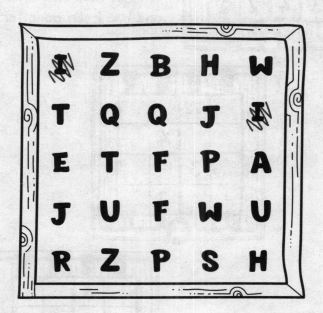

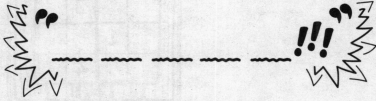

Three bears were discovered eating from the ship's food stores, and Captain Redbeak is furious! He captured the bears and locked them up in the brig, under three heavy trapdoors...

The numbers 1, 2, 3 and 4 should be added to each row, each column and each 2x2 bold outlined box, but should only appear once in each one. The first one has been done for you.

The bears are sorry, they say they were just lost and very hungry. But almost all of the crew's food for the season is now gone or ruined!

Complete the number problems on each barrel of food and write your answers into the circles. Each barrel should have the same answer. The odd one out is the only barrel left with edible food in it, but which one is it?

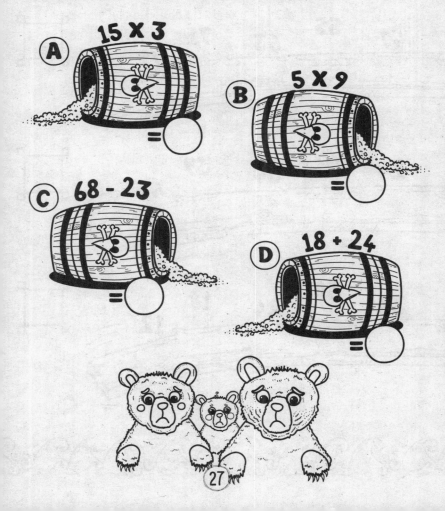

A 15 X 3 =

B 5 X 9 =

C 68 - 23 =

D 18 + 24 =

The Captain is so angry, he's going to make the bears walk the plank! But you have a feeling that the bears aren't supposed to be in this story and you decide to save them...

Follow the numbers along each plank from left to right and figure out which number is next in the sequence. Write the final numbers into the boxes at the end of the planks.

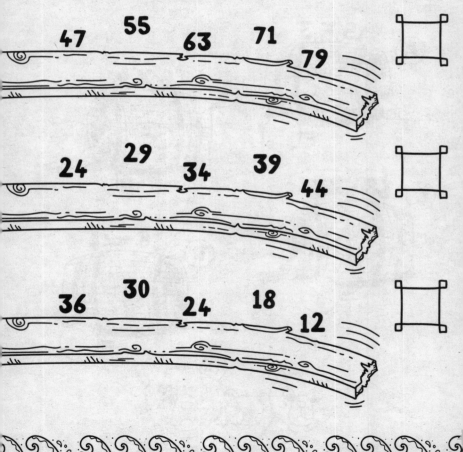

47 55 63 71 79

24 29 34 39 44

36 30 24 18 12

You walk along each plank to carefully save the bears. Once you've rescued the third bear, they slowly begin to disappear, and so do you!

But before you disappear completely, you have time to give Captain Redbeak an important message...

Use the symbol key to crack the code and fill in the gaps.

A	D	E	G	H	K	L	N	O	P	Q	R	S	T	U	Y
⚓	🛢	▲	🦴	★	⊙	ℭ	ℙ	✿	☸	☁	◇	◀	✕	🌰	⊏

"GO BACK TO THE M_ _ _ _ _ IN
      _ _ _ _ _ _ _ . FIND THE
_ _ _ _ _ _ _   _ _ _
      _ _ _ _ _ 'S _ _ _ _ _ . THERE, YOU
CAN GET M_ _ _ THAN _ _ _ _ _ _
F_ _ _ FOR YOU AND YOUR CREW
(YOU HAVE PLENTY OF _ _ _ _ _ _ _ _
NOW TO _ _ _ FOR IT!). GOOD LUCK."

29

LUE LOGBOOK:
The Pirate Story

Before you and the bears continue on your journey, take a minute to record any clues you found in the pirate story.

Remember, clues are pointed out by this symbol:

Note the clue letter next to the page number you found it on:

Page : 13   Clue letter: ◯

Page : 16   Clue letter: ◯

Page : 21   Clue letter: ◯

Page : 24   Clue letter: ◯

Page : 29   Clue letter: ◯

NOTES

(Blank 'notes' pages like this are handy for jotting down any notes or working out when you're busy solving puzzles!

You could also use them to write, doodle or anything else you'd like to do while on your quest!)

HEY DIDDLE DIDDLE!

The second story you set foot into is in the Land of Nursery Rhymes and Fables.

The three bears landed in the pirate story when Okbo's spell went wrong, but this is their real home, and they're very glad to be back here.

It's time to take on some nursery rhyme riddles and old cottage quests, plus mystery guest mind games!

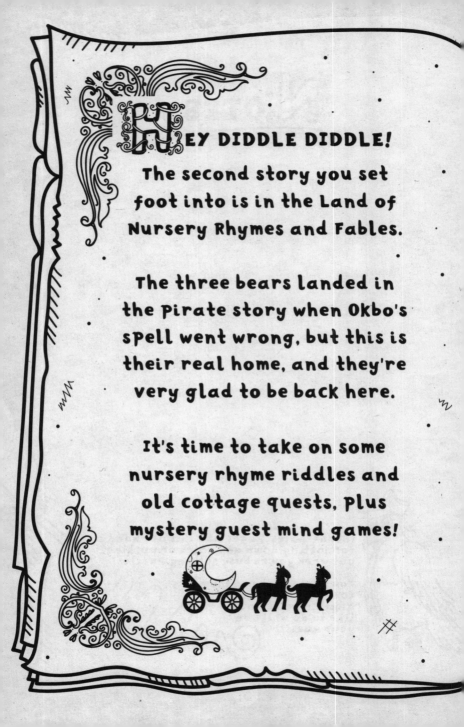

THE FABLE

The bears live in the heart of the Fabled Forest. Their home would take a long time to walk to, so you all make the journey together by moon coach instead.

What can you spy from the coach window on your trip through the forest...?

BRIDGE

COTTAGE

CREATURES

GARDEN

GATE

PATH

RIVER

TREES

Can you find all eight words from the list on the opposite page in the wordsearch below?

Words may be hidden horizontally or vertically.

```
T A S O W N M Z S J F
C I A E R S M E S E L
R T A E S R S M Z V Z
E C T W C O T T A G E
A G A B R I D G E P K
T A E A O O A T X A R
U R R I V E R R S T I
R D M S A E P E M H G
E E U O D A S E O O A
S N M I S A L S R X T
D A F P A O M O U P E
```

As you trundle deeper into the Fabled Forest, you begin to pass the houses of other characters who live in the bears' neighbourhood, like the Old Lady who Lives in a Shoe...

Can you spot all six differences between these two pictures of the Old Lady's shoe house?

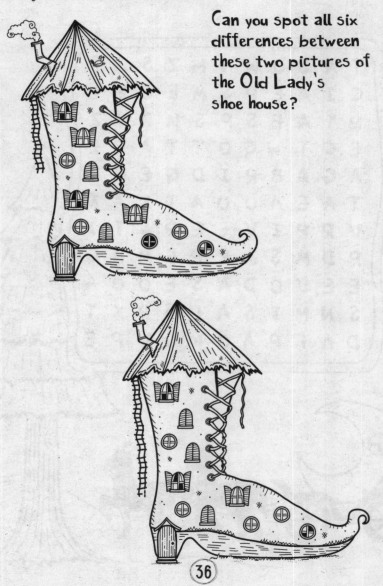

The Old Lady and all her children aren't home right now, they are out watching an exciting race between the Tortoise, the Hare, the Lion and the Mouse!

Follow the numbers down each set of footprints and figure out which number is next in the sequence. Write the final numbers into the trophies below.

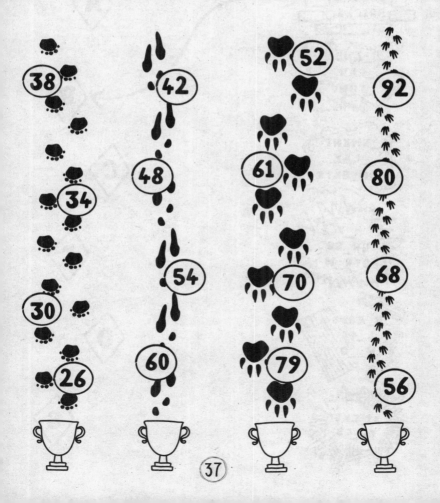

38
34
30
26

42
48
54
60

52
61
70
79

92
80
68
56

Next, you pass by the construction site where the Three Little Pigs are rebuilding their houses (yet again).

Can you match each group of building material words to the shape containing the missing letter? The first one has been done for you.

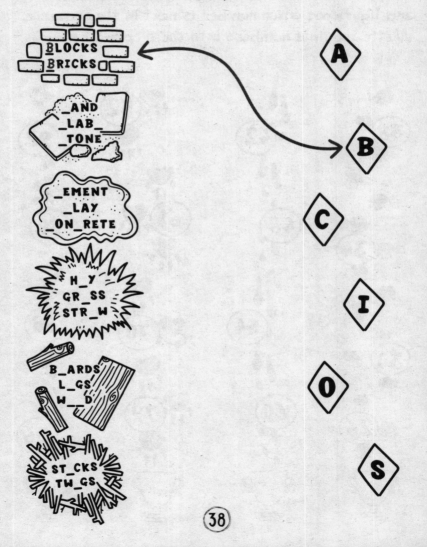

BLOCKS
BRICKS

_AND
LAB
_TONE

_EMENT
_LAY
_ON_RETE

H_Y
GR_SS
STR_W

B_ARDS
L_GS
W__D

ST_CKS
TW_GS

A

B

C

I

O

S

These piggies have tried lots of different building methods. Let's see how many huffs and puffs it would take the Big Bad Wolf to blow down each house...

Match each house's group of number problems to the cloud containing the correct answer. The first one has been done for you.

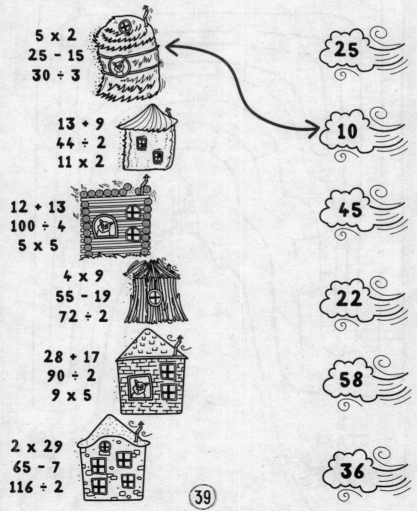

5 x 2
25 – 15
30 ÷ 3

13 + 9
44 ÷ 2
11 x 2

12 + 13
100 ÷ 4
5 x 5

4 x 9
55 – 19
72 ÷ 2

28 + 17
90 ÷ 2
9 x 5

2 x 29
65 – 7
116 ÷ 2

25

10

45

22

58

36

You're nearly there now, the bear's home is just on the other side of Jack and Jill's hill.

Can you find a way through the maze and over the hill from start to finish?

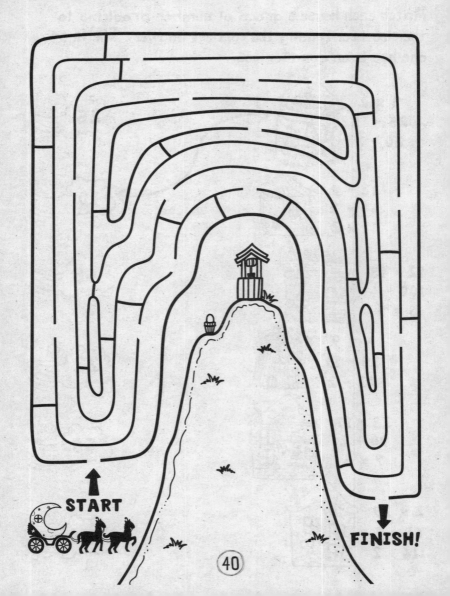

START

FINISH!

Who is that walking along looking glum? It's
Humpty Dumpty, and he has had another fall!

Can you find and circle the two correct missing
pieces to put Humpty Dumpty back together again?

After a long journey, you finally arrive at the bears' home. There are three gates to enter the garden, one entrance for each bear!

The numbers 1, 2, 3 and 4 should be added to each row, each column and each 2x2 bold outlined box, but should only appear once in each one. The first one has been done for you.

3	1	2	4
2	4	3	1
1	3	4	2
4	2	1	3

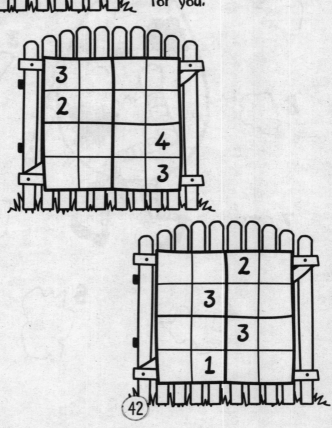

3			
2			
		4	
		3	

		2	
	3		
		3	
	1		

So, you rescued the bears from the pirate story, then brought them back to their home in the Fabled Forest. Job done, right? Wrong! The bears' front door is wide open, which means someone got to their home before they did. Hmm, another mystery for you to solve...

Follow the tangled garden paths. Which one leads you to the open front door?

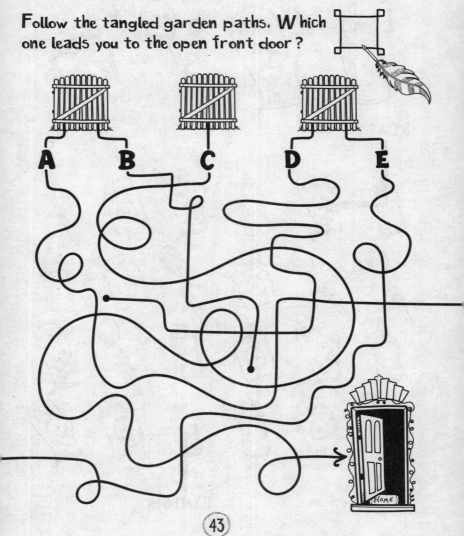

You start in the bears' kitchen, looking for clues...

Make your way from start to finish. You can move up, down or sideways but you can't move diagonally and you must follow the kitchen items in this order:

There should only be three bowls on the table, but there are four! What has the mysterious intruder been eating?

Unscramble the letters in the bowls to reveal what kind of food is inside each one. Some letters have already been done for you.

In the bears' living room, there are usually only three chairs – one small, one medium and one large.

Which silhouette correctly matches each chair? Circle your answers.

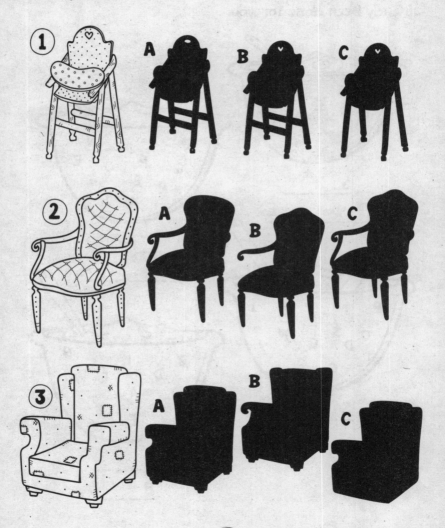

In the bears' bedroom, there are usually only three beds – one small, one medium and one large.

Which silhouette correctly matches each bed? Circle your answers.

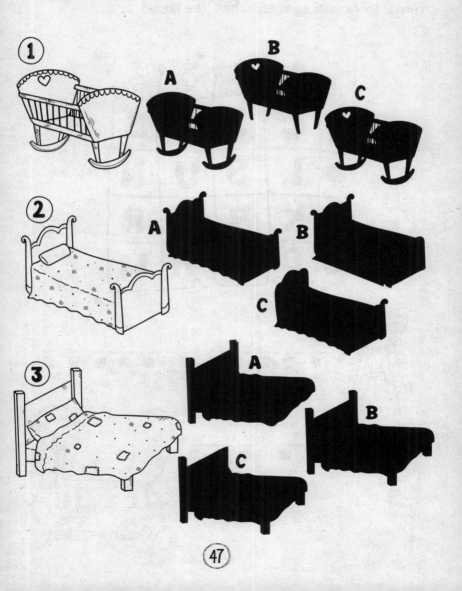

Now, there is a fourth chair in the bears' living room and a fourth bed in the bears' bedroom! They don't quite fit in here.

Use the symbol Key to crack the code and fill in the gaps to reveal exactly what the items are...

1   2   3   4

★ G I T E
■ L S U N
● K B A R
🌀 D O H W

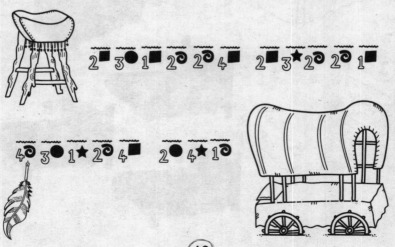

2■ 3● 1■ 2○ 2○ 4■   2■ 3★ 2○ 2○ 1■

4○ 3● 1★ 2○ 4■ ■   2○ 4★ 1○

Everything else in the bears' bedroom seems to be quite normal, for now...

In the word-wheels, find three common things you might find in a bedroom. Each word starts with the centre letter and uses all the letters in the wheel once.

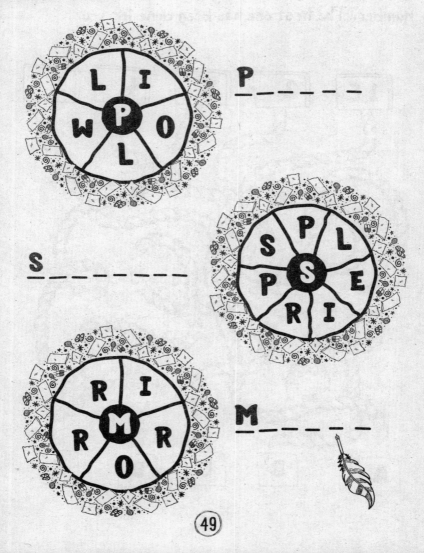

P _ _ _ _ _

S _ _ _ _ _ _ _ _

M _ _ _ _ _ _

Then, in the corner of the room, you notice a mess of ropes... it looks like someone has been trying to lasso items from the shelves and has knocked some of the bears' belongings over!

Can you untangle the ropes? Follow each one and write the correct matching letter next to each rope number. The first one has been done for you.

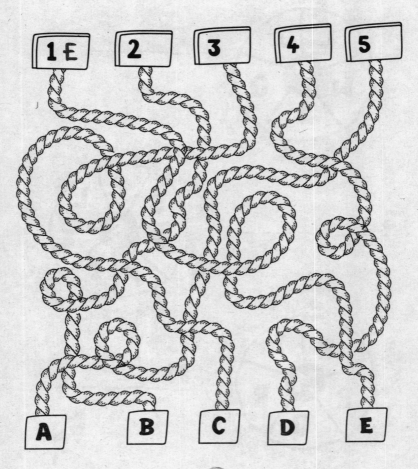

That's when you spot them – the muddy boot prints!

Can you find a path to follow the boot prints from start to finish, only going in the direction of the arrows?

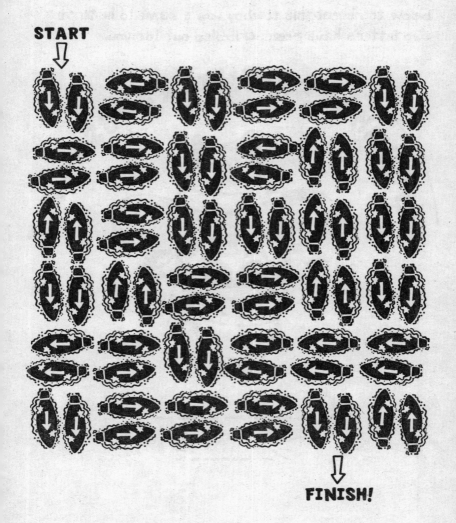

START

FINISH!

The muddy boot prints lead you to quite the surprise... a cowboy cow has been living in the bears' home!

Scribble out every other letter from left to right. Write the letters that are left over on the lines below to reveal this cowboy cow's name. The first two letters have been scribbled out for you.

S C F O U W H A K B R U I N J G K A P B S I Q L Y L Z

C _ _ _ _ _ _ _ _ _ _

_ _ _ _ _

Solve the number problem below each letter in the Key. Then use the answers to fill in the gaps and find out what happens next. Some letters have already been done for you.

A	B	D	E	G	I	L	N
3+6	23-8	6×4	5×6	6×3	14÷2	25÷5	18÷9
	15						

O	P	R	S	T	U	W	Y
11+3	9-5	3×4	4×2	11×2	24÷4	40÷2	21÷7
			8				

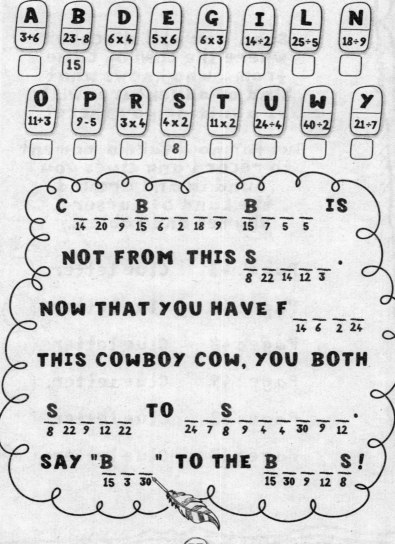

C _ _ _ B _ _ _ B _ _ _ IS
 14 20 9 15 6 2 18 9 15 7 5 5

NOT FROM THIS S _ _ _ _ .
                8 22 14 12 3

NOW THAT YOU HAVE F _ _ _ _
                     14 6 2 24

THIS COWBOY COW, YOU BOTH

S _ _ _ _   TO _ S _ _ _ _ _ _ _ .
8 22 9 12 22   24 7 8 9 4 4 30 9 12

SAY "B _ _" TO THE B _ _ _ _ S!
     15 3 30   15 30 9 12 8

LUE LOGBOOK:
The Fable

Soon, you will discover where the cowboy came from – who knows what kind of adventures will be awaiting you there?

But for now, take a moment to record any clues you found in and around the Land of Nursery Rhymes and Fables...

Page : 43   Clue letter: ◯

Page : 45   Clue letter: ◯

Page : 48   Clue letter: ◯

Page : 49   Clue letter: ◯

Page : 52   Clue letter: ◯

Page : 53   Clue letter: ◯

NOTES

HOWDY PARTNER!

Are you ready for a rootin' tootin' time? You are on your way into the Cowboy Story where Cowabunga Bill lives.

Giddy up and get ready for plenty of wild west word puzzles, mine cart mind games and cowboy quests!

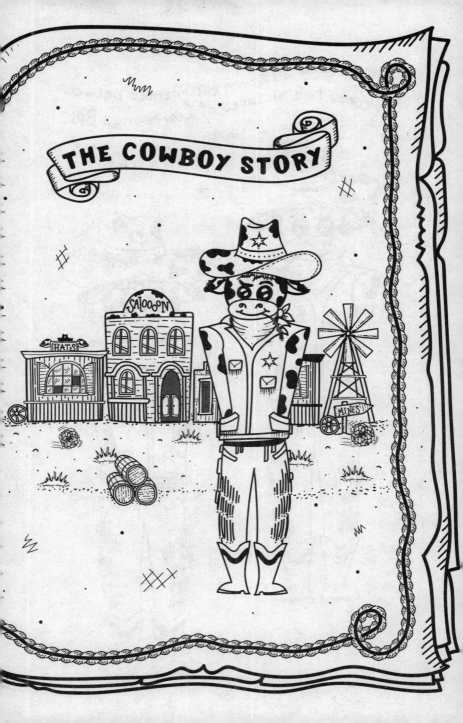

Can you spot all seven differences between these two pictures of Cowabunga Bill?

Cowabunga Bill is the sheriff of his town.

Which silhouettes correctly match the sheriff's hat, badge and boots? Circle your answers.

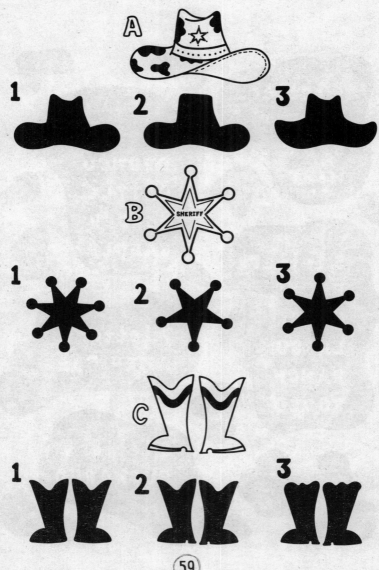

You ride into town with Cowabunga Bill on horseback. You've never seen a cowboy cow riding a horse before... it sure is a strange sight to see!

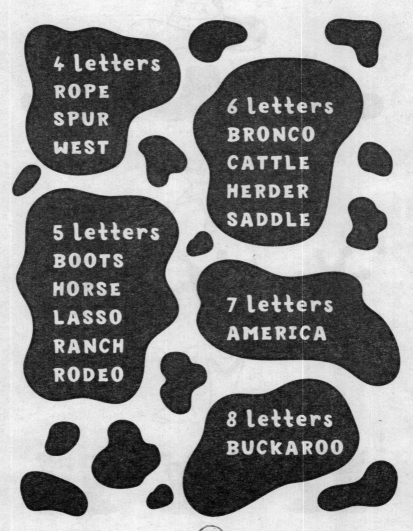

4 letters
ROPE
SPUR
WEST

6 letters
BRONCO
CATTLE
HERDER
SADDLE

5 letters
BOOTS
HORSE
LASSO
RANCH
RODEO

7 letters
AMERICA

8 letters
BUCKAROO

Place each of the cowboy words from the list on the opposite page into the empty squares to create a filled crossword grid. Each word is used once so cross it off the list as you place it to help you keep track.

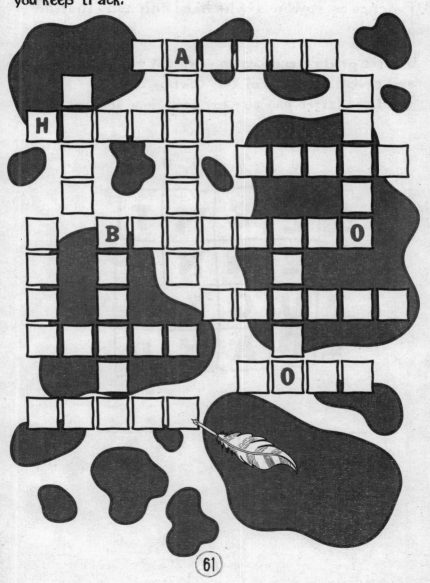

This small and dusty desert town has a population of just 400... and they are all cows! Most of the cows who live here work in the town's gold mines, in the shops and saloons, or on the ranches as 'cowboys' who herd chickens instead of cattle!

Use the grid references to work out each letter and reveal the name of this cowboy town.
The first letter has already been done for you.

Can you spot all eight differences between these two pictures of the town?

If you want to fit in in this town, you'll need to find yourself a hat! Let's visit the local hat shop, where they don't just sell cowboy hats – there are all different kinds to choose from! Which one will you pick?

Can you find all eight hats from the list on the opposite page in the wordsearch below? Words may be hidden horizontally or vertically.

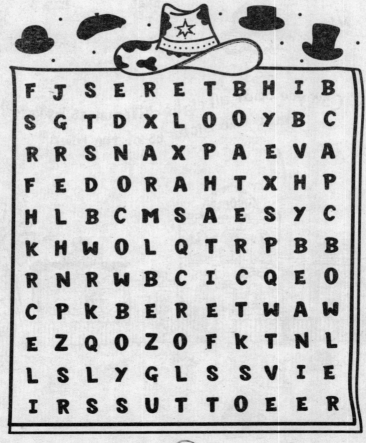

```
F J S E R E T B H I B
S G T D X L O O Y B C
R R S N A X P A E V A
F E D O R A H T X H P
H L B C M S A E S Y C
K H W O L Q T R P B B
R N R W B C I C Q E O
C P K B E R E T W A W
E Z Q O Z O F K T N L
L S L Y G L S S V I E
I R S S U T T O E R R
```

BEANIE

BERET

BOATER

BOWLER

CAP

COWBOY

FEDORA

TOP HAT

After you've bought the perfect hat, you and the sheriff go to the saloon bar for some juice. Hat shopping is thirsty work in this desert heat!

In the word-wheels, find three things you might find inside the saloon. Each word starts with the centre letter and uses all the letters in the wheel once.

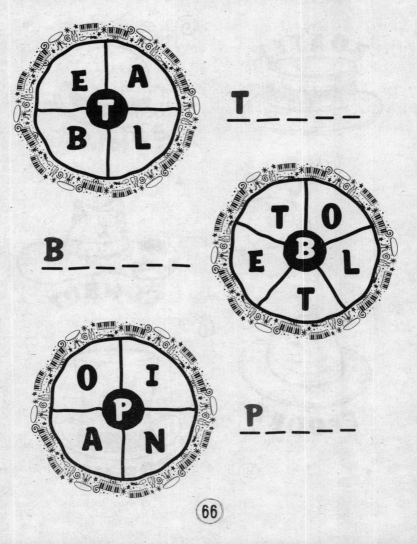

T _ _ _ _ _

B _ _ _ _ _ _

P _ _ _ _ _

The saloon is completely deserted apart from the cow working there, who is very glad to see you and the sheriff walking in – you're their first customers in days!

What has happened here? There are clues on the walls...

Cross out any letter that appears more than once in the grid below. Write the letters that are left over on the lines below in the order they appear, and a hidden word will reveal itself. Letter V has been scribbled out to start you off.

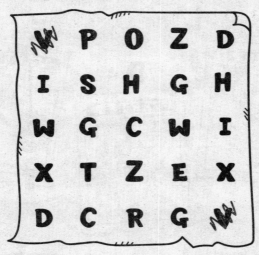

V	P	O	Z	D
I	S	H	G	H
W	G	C	W	I
X	T	Z	E	X
D	C	R	G	V

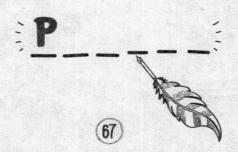

P _ _ _ _ _

There are wanted posters all over the saloon walls!

Odd one out: which wanted poster does not have a matching pair? Circle your answer.

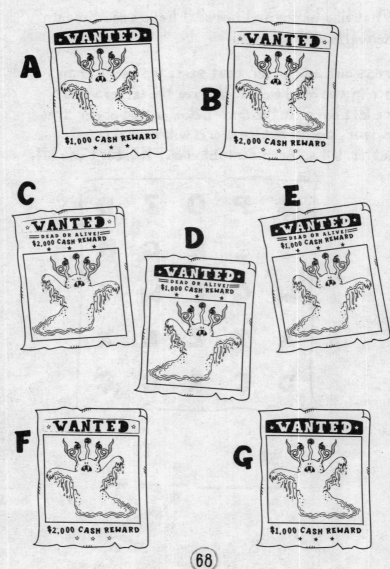

The saloon cow tells you all about the monster who arrived in town not long ago and has already caused a lot of problems that need sorting. It's lucky you brought the sheriff back when you did!

Use the symbol key to crack the code and fill in the gaps to reveal four things the monster has done...

A	C	D	E	I	L	M	N	O	P	R	S	T	U	W

1. _ _ _ _ _ _ MOST OF THE B _ _ _

_ _ _ _ _ _ IN WILDMOO RIDGE!

2. _ _ _ _ _ _ _ ALL THE _ _ _ _ _ _ _ _ _

AWAY FROM THE _ _ _ _ _ _ .

3. _ _ _ _ _ _ _ ALL THE _ _ _ _ _ _ _ _

AWAY FROM THE G _ _ _ _ _ _ _ _ .

4. RUINED THE _ _ _ _ _ BY GETTING

_ _ _ _ _ IN THE WILDMOO _ _ _ _ !

69

The monster should be easy enough to find – it leaves a trail of slime wherever it goes! No one has been brave enough to follow it yet. That is, until you and Cowabunga Bill showed up...

The monster has left lots of slime trails all over town, but the most recent one leads all the way to the gold mines... which one is it?

WILDMOO GOLD MINES

The slime trail doesn't just lead you to the gold mine entrance, it goes further, deep down into the mines!

Can you find a way down through the maze from 'start' at the mine entrance, to 'finish' deep down in the caverns?

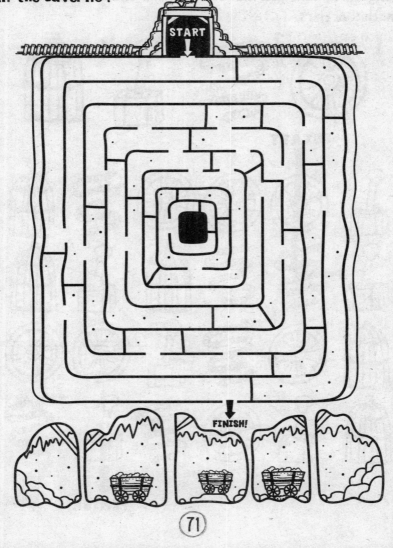

You can hear the monster clanging around down in the mines. It's time for you and the sheriff to set up a monster trap!

Make your way from start to finish. You can move up, down or sideways but you can't move diagonally and you must follow the trap equipment in this order:

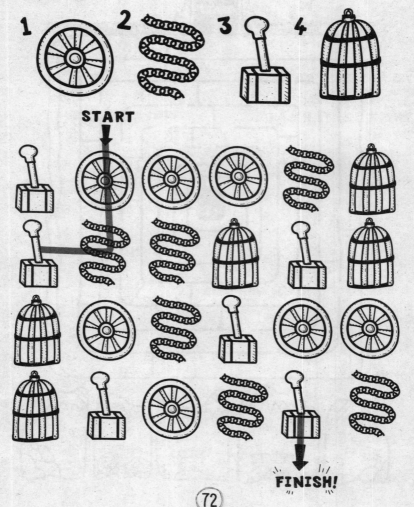

Solve the number problem below each letter in the Key. Then use the answers to fill in the gaps and reveal what happens. Some letters have been done for you.

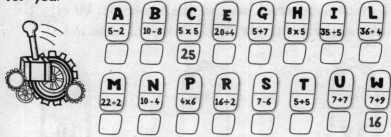

A	B	C	E	G	H	I	L
5−2	10−8	5 × 5	20÷4	5+7	8 × 5	35 ÷ 5	36 ÷ 4
		25					

M	N	P	R	S	T	U	W
22÷2	10−4	4×6	16÷2	7−6	5+5	7+7	7+9
							16

YOU SET A TRAP THEN W _ _ _ _ AND W _ _ _,
            16 3 10 25 40   16 3 7 10

THE MONSTER EATS _ _ _ _ _ YOU SET AS _ _ _ _.
            2 5 3 6 1   2 3 7 10

YOU PULL THE _ _ V _ _ AT THE RIGHT _ _ _ _,
          9 5   5 8   10 7 11 5

DOWN COMES A C _ _ _ _ TO TRAP THE _ _ _ _ _.
          25 3 12 5   1 9 7 11 5

THE MONSTER IS C _ _ _ _ _ _ WITHIN THE C _ _ _,
          25 3 14 12 40 10   25 3 8 10

SO YOU AND THE SHERIFF J _ _ _ _ _
                   14 11 24 7 6

AND D _ _ _ _ _ _.
    5 24 3 8 10

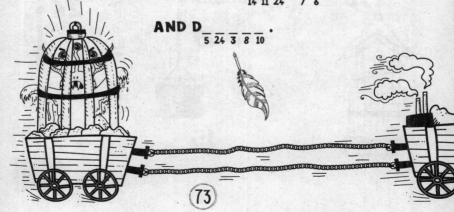

73

Now you have captured the monster, can you get it up and out of the mines before it breaks free?

Follow the numbers up each mine elevator and figure out which number is next in the sequence. Write the final numbers into the cogs at top of each lift.

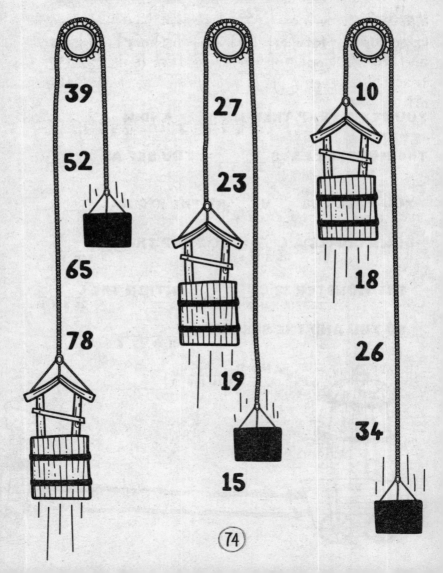

39
52
65
78

27
23
19
15

10
18
26
34

You and the sheriff made it back up to the surface with the monster in tow. Phew! Use the mine railway to take the monster back into Wildmoo Ridge, where you can decide what to do next with it.

Make your way from start to finish. You can move up, down or sideways, but you can't move diagonally and you must only follow the mine carts or railway tracks with even numbers. The line has been started off for you.

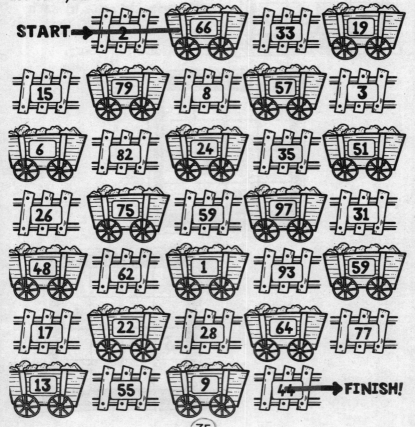

The residents of Wildmoo Ridge are so relieved you have finally captured the monster that has been ruining their lives! They want to see the monster imprisoned behind bars in the county jail...

4	2	3	1
3	1	4	2
2	3	1	4
1	4	2	3

The numbers 1, 2, 3 and 4 should be added to each row, each column and each 2x2 bold outlined box, but should only appear once in each one. The first one has been done for you.

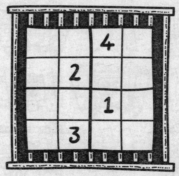

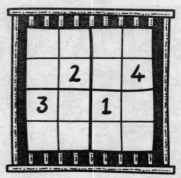

You explain to the cows of Wildmoo Ridge that the monster belongs to another story, so they can't imprison it forever. They allow you to take the monster back to its real home, but first, they want to do something to celebrate and thank you...

Scribble out every other letter from left to right. Write the letters that are left over on the lines below. The first four letters have been scribbled out for you.

YTOSUEARBEFMGAHDJEKDFEDPBUYTTYSSGHVEB
RNIMFEFWOQFSTXHZEATDORWYNUAJNBDFGWIOV
PENNKANSRHSIENYYUBNAGDDGFE

YOU A__ ____ _____

_____ __ ____

___ _____ _

_____ ____!

LUE LOGBOOK:
The Cowboy Story

Yee haw, that was quite
an adventure!

So, sheriff, what now?

In just a moment, it will be
time to take the monster
back to its spooky home.

But before you go, note
down any clues you found
in the dusty desert town
of Wildmoo Ridge...

Page : 61   Clue letter: ◯

Page : 62   Clue letter: ◯

Page : 67   Clue letter: ◯

Page : 70   Clue letter: ◯

Page : 73   Clue letter: ◯

NOTES

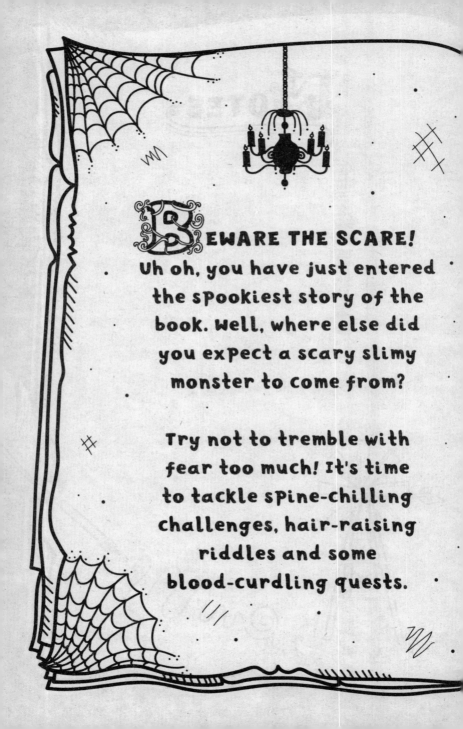

BEWARE THE SCARE!

Uh oh, you have just entered the spookiest story of the book. Well, where else did you expect a scary slimy monster to come from?

Try not to tremble with fear too much! It's time to tackle spine-chilling challenges, hair-raising riddles and some blood-curdling quests.

THE SPOOKY STORY

You were hoping to get to know the monster better so you could have a tour guide to show you round the spooky town. Alas, monsters are not known for their hosting skills! The minute you arrive, the slimy monster slithers away!

So, here you are, left all alone in a dark and scary town, where the air is cold, leaves crunch underfoot, and you can hear howling in the distance...

CHILLY

CREEPY

DARK

EERIE

FRIGHTENING

GHOSTLY

SCARY

SPOOKY

You try to remind yourself that it's only a story, as you walk through the darkness.

"It's just a story, it's not real, it's just a story..."

Can you find all eight spooky atmoshphere words from the list on the opposite page in the wordsearch below? Words may be hidden horizontally or vertically.

O C R L X M X N R T V
A R G F Q K J T W Y O
T E H U R E E R I E C
S E O U D G B I E O D
C P S L C H I L L Y D
A Y T Q Z X B R I U R
R P L L X S P O O K Y
Y Y Y I C T C R I S T
F R I G H T E N I N G
P M R S S U F V F I W
D A R K S I B L Y Z U

You find yourself in a graveyard. It's far too scary. Quick, run through as fast as you can!

Follow the lines and write the letter from each circle in the space at the end of each line to reveal a new word. The first letter of each word has already been done for you.

Complete the number problems below and write your answers into the boxes. Each gravestone should have the same answer. The odd one out is the grave you should avoid going past because a ghoul is waiting behind it to pop out and scare you, agh!
Which one is it?

W 33 x 2 =

X 100 - 36 =

Y 132 ÷ 2 =

Z 3 x 22 =

The town is filled with tall pumpkin towers that loom over you while you explore, watching you with their creepy faces...

Follow the numbers up each pumpkin tower and figure out which number is next in the sequence. Write the final numbers into the circles at the top of the towers.

You spot some not-so-familiar characters here, like a vampire otter selling some very strange things...

Can you find all eight items from the list in the wordsearch? Words may be hidden in the grid horizontally or vertically.

- BATS • BLOOD
- CANDLES • COBWEBS
- FANGS • FINGERS
- SKELETONS
- SPIDERS

T	A	S	O	W	N	M	Z	S	J	F	C	F
C	I	P	E	R	S	M	E	S	E	L	A	L
R	F	I	N	G	E	R	S	Z	V	Z	N	Z
E	C	D	W	B	L	O	O	D	G	E	D	E
A	G	E	B	R	J	D	G	E	P	K	L	K
F	P	R	A	O	O	A	T	X	A	R	E	R
A	R	S	T	V	C	O	B	W	E	B	S	I
N	D	M	S	A	E	P	E	M	H	G	H	G
G	E	U	O	D	A	S	E	O	O	A	O	A
S	K	E	L	E	T	O	N	S	X	T	X	T

On an eerie construction site, you recognise three zombie pigs who are rebuilding their houses (again) with some pretty creepy materials!

Can you match each group of building material words to the shape containing the missing letter?

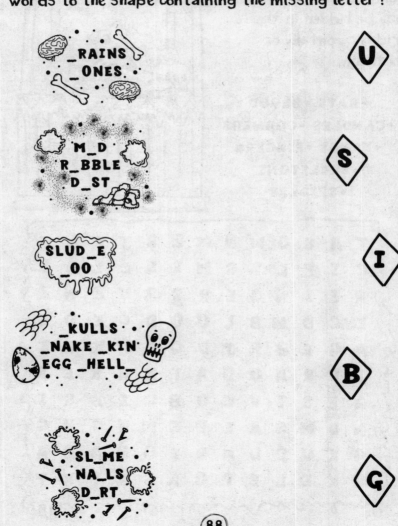

_RAINS
_ONES

U

M_D
R_BBLE
D_ST

S

SLUD_E
_OO

I

_KULLS
_NAKE _KIN
EGG _HELL_

B

SL_ME
NA_LS
D_RT

G

You also walk by a haunted saloon, where the ghosts of 400 cows are howling, wailing and mooo-aning!

Odd one out: which ghost cow does not have an identical twin? Circle your answer.

This story is home to all kinds of weird and wonderful, creepy and spooky creatures.

Some are wandering around, doing their day-to-day hair-raising activities. But you also see lots of them running... running away from something...

What could they be running from?

3 letters
BAT

4 letters
OGRE

5 letters
DEMON
DEVIL
GHOUL
MUMMY
TROLL

6 letters
GOBLIN
KRAKEN
SPIDER

7 letters
BANSHEE
GREMLIN

8 letters
BASILISK

Place each of the creature words from the list on the
opposite page into the empty squares to create
a filled crossword grid. Each word is used once
so cross it off the list as you place it to help you
keep track.

You walk towards where the creatures were running from and you find an old haunted house on a hill. What's inside that house must be truly terrifying if it scared all those monsters away!

Can you spot all seven differences between these two pictures of the haunted house?

At that moment, you hear a terrible screeching noise! It seems the town wailer is making an emergency news announcement...

Scribble out every other letter from left to right. Write the letters that are left over on the lines below to reveal the announcement. The first seven letters have been scribbled out for you.

UERBGEEWNETRTDHSEEHWAAUFNGTHEJD
KHLOBUCSXESIASWOTFRFELWIQMXIVTFS
GUHNSTVIBLWTXHYESFGAJIKRLYBCNAYT
MCEHWESRFHAAPSLVMIXSZIATQERD

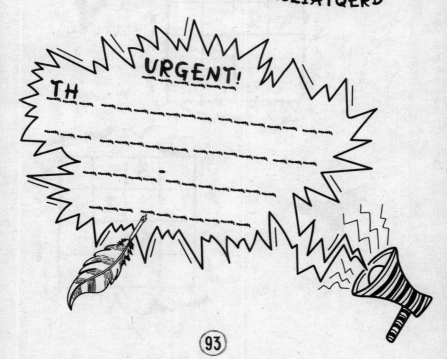

URGENT!

TH _____

_____

_____

_____ - _____

_____

The loud announcement sends hundreds of bats flying and squeaking through the air!

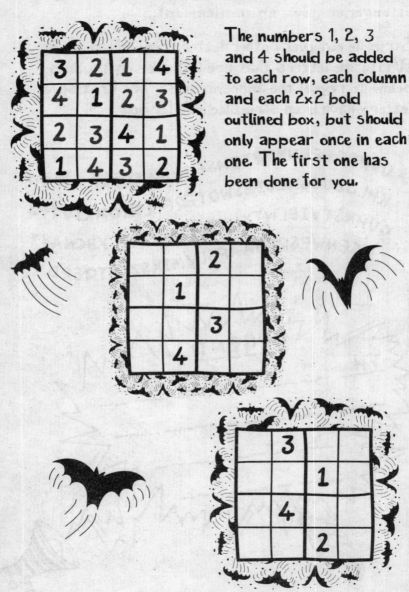

The numbers 1, 2, 3 and 4 should be added to each row, each column and each 2x2 bold outlined box, but should only appear once in each one. The first one has been done for you.

3	2	1	4
4	1	2	3
2	3	4	1
1	4	3	2

A small, fierce-looking goblin approaches you and says, "That was quick! You must be the fairy-catcher, follow me!" You don't really want to argue, so you follow as the goblin marches off...

Follow the tangled paths. Which one is the route the goblin takes?

The goblin leads you up the hill and into...
the haunted house. Uh oh!

Can you make your way through the maze from
start to finish in the centre of the haunted house?

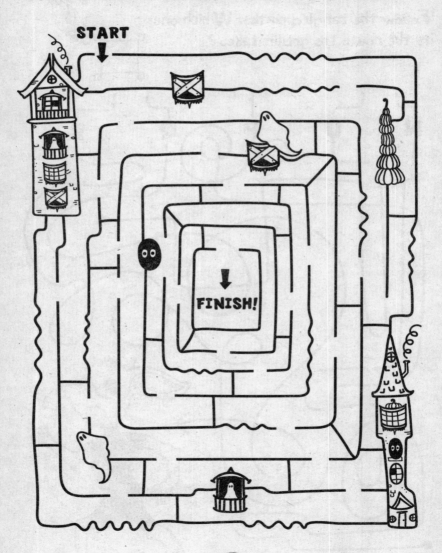

START

FINISH!

It's certainly an old, creaky and creepy house, but you haven't seen anything TOO terrifying yet... what could have scared all those monsters away like that?

In the word-wheels, find three things you might find inside a haunted house. Each word starts with the centre letter and uses all the letters in the wheel once.

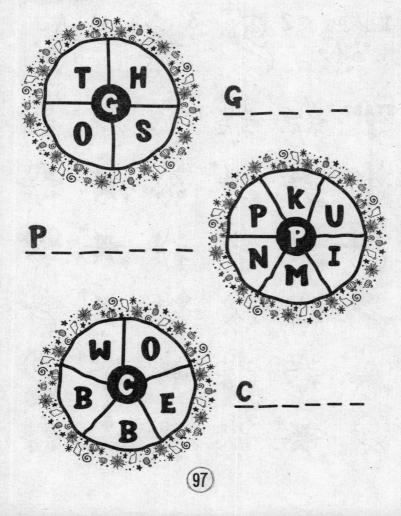

G _ _ _ _ _

P _ _ _ _ _ _

C _ _ _ _ _ _

The goblin stops and says, shivering, "H-h-here is the trail of f-f-f-fairy dust... I can go no further." Suddenly you realise... all of these monsters are terrified of a fairy!

Make your way from start to finish. You can move up, down or sideways but you can't move diagonally and you must follow the fairy dust in this order:

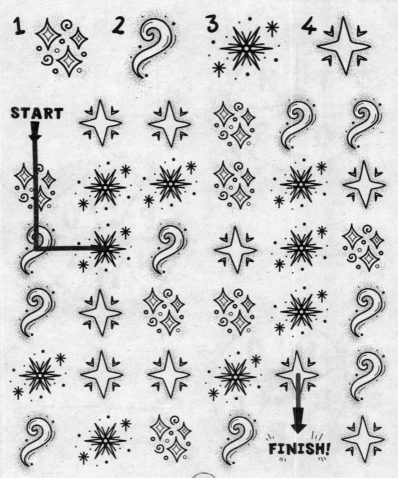

As you follow the trail of fairy dust, you start to pass by evidence of all the 'scary' things the fairy has been doing to this part of the haunted house.

Solve the number problem below each letter in the Key. Then use the answers to fill in the gaps. One letter has been done for you.

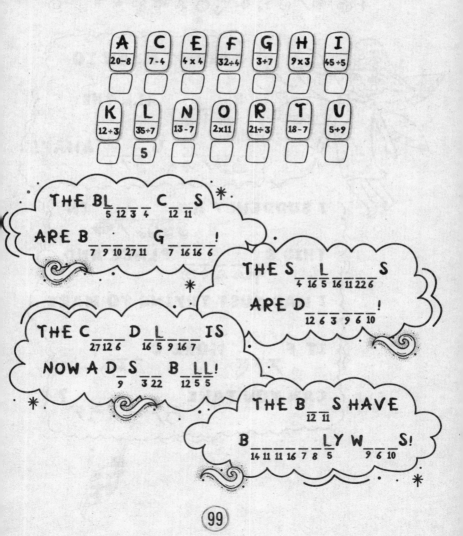

Key:

A	C	E	F	G	H	I
20−8	7−4	4×4	32÷4	3+7	9×3	45÷5

K	L	N	O	R	T	U
12÷3	35÷7	13−7	2×11	21÷3	18−7	5+9

L = 5

THE BL _ _ _ _ C _ S
    5 12 3 4   12 11

ARE B _ _ _ _ _ G _ _ _ !
     7 9 10 27 11   7 16 16 6

THE S _ _ L _ _ _ S
      4 16 5 16 11 22 6

ARE D _ _ _ _ _ !
      12 6 3 9 6 10

THE C _ _ _ D _ L _ _ _ IS
      27 12 6   16 5 9 16 7

NOW A D _ S _ _ B _ LL!
        9   3 22   12 5 5

THE B _ _ S HAVE
      12 11

B _ _ _ _ _ _ LY W _ _ S!
  14 11 11 16 7 8 5   9 6 10

You finally find the culprit: a mushroom fairy!

Use the symbol Key to crack the code and fill in the gaps to reveal what the fairy tells you...

A C D E H I K L M O P R S T V Y

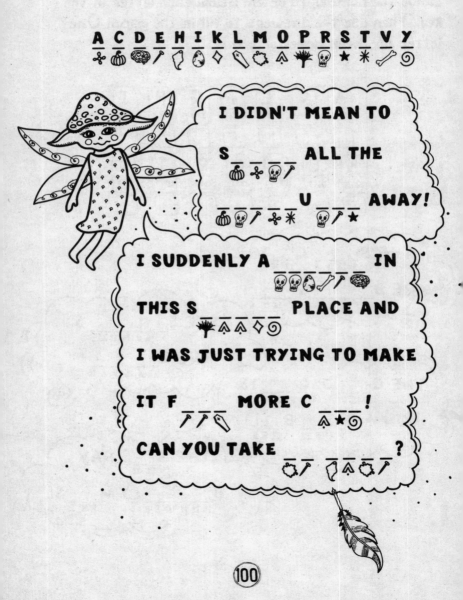

I DIDN'T MEAN TO

S _ _ _ ALL THE

_ _ _ _ _ U _ _ _ AWAY!

I SUDDENLY A _ _ _ _ _ _ IN

THIS S _ _ _ _ _ PLACE AND

I WAS JUST TRYING TO MAKE

IT F _ _ _ MORE C _ _ _ !

CAN YOU TAKE _ _ _ _ _ _ _ ?

You both begin to disappear. Before you leave this story completely, fly around with the fairy and help them restore the haunted house's spookiness so the creatures can return!

Make your way from start to finish. You can move up, down or sideways, but you can't move diagonally and you must only follow the items with odd numbers. The line has been started off for you.

START

FINISH!

 LUE LOGBOOK:
The Spooky Story

Phew, aren't you glad to get out of there!?

You and your new mushroom fairy friend, called Amanita, are about to enter the final chapter of this amazing journey...

But first, take time to record any clues you found while exploring that spooky-ooky town.

Page : 85   Clue letter: ◯

Page : 91   Clue letter: ◯

Page : 93   Clue letter: ◯

Page : 95   Clue letter: ◯

Page : 100   Clue letter: ◯

NOTES

ONCE UPON A TIME...

You stepped into the pages of an old story book, met some curious characters, helped them return to the stories they came from, and then ended up here, at the final story: the fairytale.

Prepare yourself for a world of magical mind games, mushroom mysteries, and enchanted challenges.

Amanita can fly at incredibly high speeds, and needs to, because home is far, far away from here!

But Amanita isn't strong enough to carry you all the way, so you'll be joined by a friend who can help you keep up with the fairy as you travel across the land...

Can you find and circle the complete word 'UNICORN' hidden in the bubble below?

This enormous but shy and gentle beast will be your travel companion as you follow Amanita home.

Scribble out every other letter from left to right. Write the letters that are left over on the lines below to reveal your new friend's name. The first two letters have already been done for you.

S H _ _ _ _ _ _

_ _ _ _ _ _ _ _

_ _ _ _

You and your new unicorn friend follow Amanita across the bridges into this fantasy fairytale land.

Follow the numbers along each bridge from left to right and figure out which number is next in the sequence. Write the final numbers into the circles.

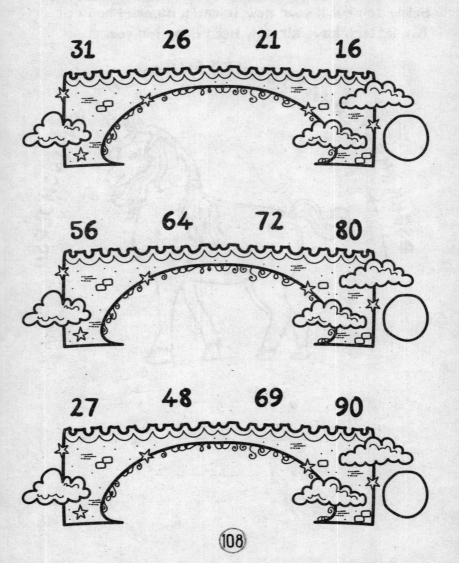

31   26   21   16

56   64   72   80

27   48   69   90

You travel past a tall tower where Rapunzel has had a haircut. The hair that's still attached to her head is all tangled up in the hair from her haircut!

Can you help? Follow the tangled plaits. Which one flows all the way from Rapunzel inside the tower?

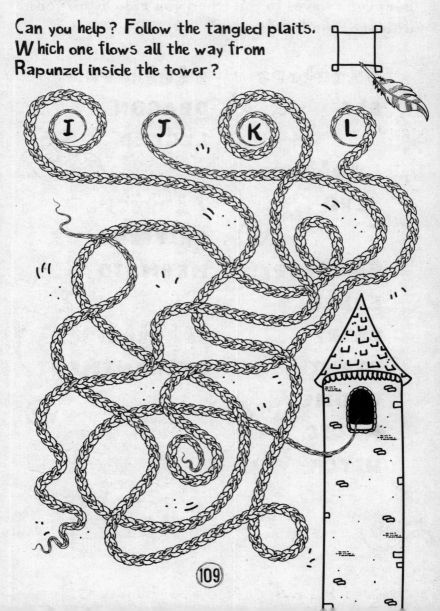

This story is home to plenty of magical characters, you wish you had the chance to stop and meet them all.

Everyone waves to you when you ride by on your unicorn, you feel famous!

3 letters

ELF

4 letters

HERO

5 letters

FABLE

FAIRY

GIANT

GNOME

MAGIC

WITCH

6 letters

DRAGON

LEGEND

7 letters

GRIFFIN

MERMAID

11 letters

ENCHANTMENT

Place each of the fairytale words from the list on the opposite page into the empty squares to create a filled crossword grid. Each word is used once so cross it off the list as you place it to help you keep track.

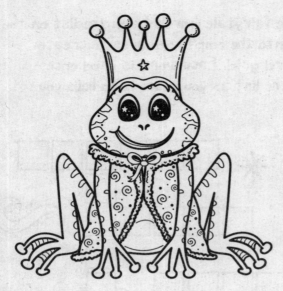

You soon reach an enormous pond guarded by a charming frog prince.

Can you spot all six differences between these two pictures of the frog prince?

Amanita flies across, but you must leave your friend Shabira the unicorn here, as you'll need to hop across the giant lilypads on foot.

Make your way from start to finish. You can move up, down or sideways, but you can't move diagonally and you must only follow the lilypads with even numbers. The line has been started off for you.

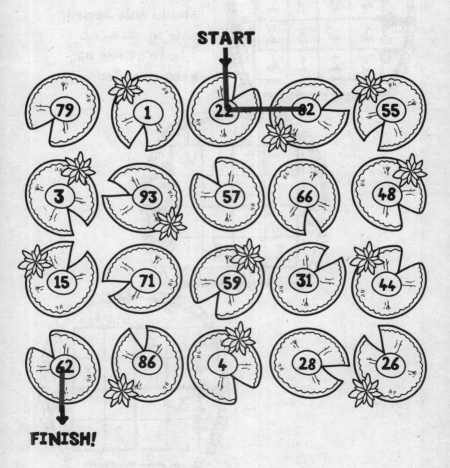

START

79 1 22 82 55

3 93 57 66 48

15 71 59 31 44

62 86 4 28 26

FINISH!

On the other side of the pond, you find a forest of trees with curious little doors in each trunk.

The numbers 1, 2, 3 and 4 should be added to each row, each column and each 2x2 bold outlined box, but should only appear once in each one. The first one has been done for you.

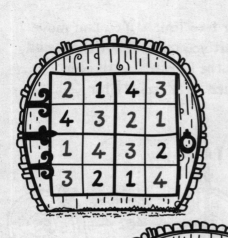

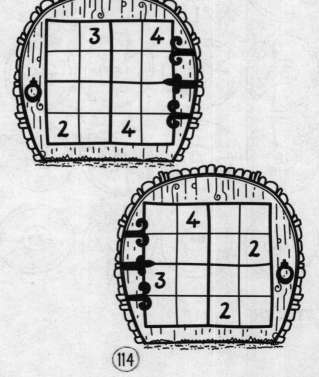

You follow Amanita through one of the tree doors and find yourself in a clearing with a large circle of mushrooms in the middle...

Odd one out: which mushroom does not have a matching twin?

As you step into the middle of the mushroom circle, it suddenly springs to life! You realise you are standing amongst Amanita and the rest of their mushroom fairy friends, who are all named after types of mushroom.

Can you find all mushroom fairy names from the list on the opposite page in the wordsearch below? Words may be hidden horizontally or vertically.

```
U U A M A N I T A P L
S F K H E D G E H O G
C H A N T E R E L L E
B C A B Z P J R U C A
T A P T M O Q U J R B
Q C A N A R Q T S E U
F R K W T C O H L M T
M O R E L I P M A I T
C H E S T N U T S N O
H A K E Z I U R E I N
S O E E L I W R R R M
```

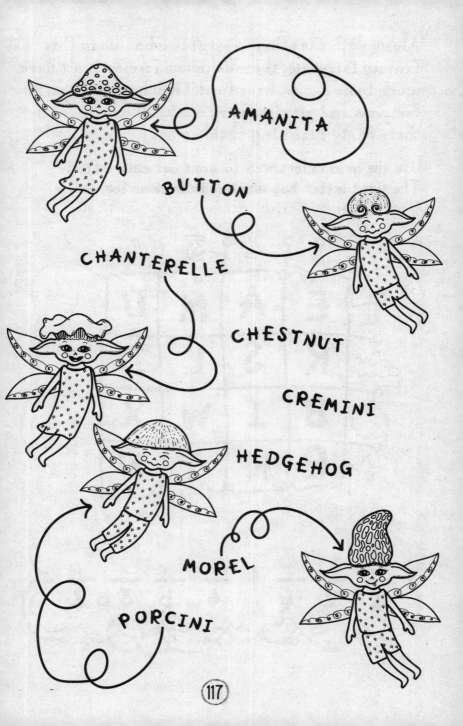

AMANITA

BUTTON

CHANTERELLE

CHESTNUT

CREMINI

HEDGEHOG

MOREL

PORCINI

Along with the other creatures who live in this fantasy fairytale, the mushroom fairies don't have much to do except have fun! They have parties, festivals and picnics every week, all organised by their Party Planning Club.

Use the grid references to work out each letter. The first letter has already been done for you.

B

Before disappearing, Amanita was Head of the Party Planning Club and planned LOTS of woodland-themed parties. But now, the other fairies in the club have something to say...

Solve the number problem below each letter in the Key. Then use the answers to fill in the gaps and reveal what the fairies tell Amanita. Some letters have already been done for you.

A	B	D	E	F	H	I
25−6	9−4	8 × 3	44÷4	7+7	9×4	45÷5
			11			

N	O	R	S	T	W	Y
30÷2	30÷5	12−9	2×8	20÷2	20−8	5+8

S _ _ _ AMANITA. WHILE YOU WERE G _ _ E
  6 3 3 13   6 15 11

SOMEONE _ E _ CAME ALONG WITH LOTS OF FUN
        15 11 12

P _ _ _ _ _ _ E _ _ . WE _ _ _ E _ THEM AS THE
  19 3 10 13 9 24 11 19 16   36 9 3 11 24

_ E _ _ E _ _ _ OF THE CLUB. BUT YOU C _ _ _ GET
15 11 12 36 11 19 24   19 15

YOUR J _ _ BACK IF YOU THINK OF SOME _ E _
       6 5   15 11 12

P _ _ _ _ _ E M E _ THAT ARE FUN AND _ _ E _ _ !
  19 3 10 13 10 36 11 11 16   14 3 11 16 36

The fairies take you to meet the new Head of the Party Planning Club. To your surprise, it's the missing 20th member of Captain Redbeak's parrot pirate crew!

Which silhouette correctly matches the parrot pirate party planner?

(A)

(H)

(O)

(Y)

The pirate has planned a beach-themed party.
The fairies are very excited, they've only ever
been to woodland-themed parties before!

Can you make your way to the beach party,
through the maze from start to finish?

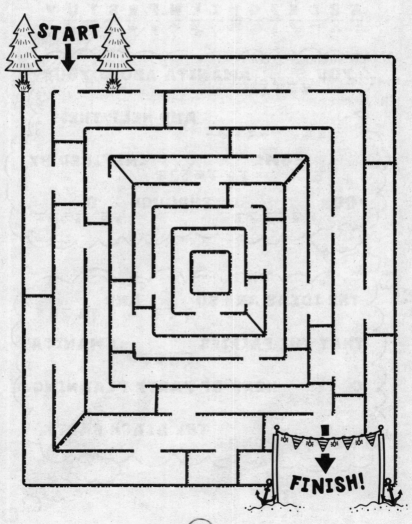

Before you can enjoy the party, you need to help Amanita get their job back!

Use the symbol key to crack the code and fill in the gaps to reveal how you help...

A B D E F G H I L N P R S T U V

YOU _ _ _ _ AMANITA ABOUT YOUR

_ _ _ _ _ _ _ _ _ _ AND HELP THEM

_ _ _ _ _ SOME _ _ _ _ _ _ INSPIRED BY

YOUR _ _ _ _ _ _ _ _ THROUGH _ O _ _ _ .

THE IDEAS ARE SO _ _ _ AND _ _ _ _ _

THAT THE FAIRIES _ _ _ _ _ AMANITA

C _ _ _ _ HEAD OF PARTY PLANNING

_ _ _ _ _ _ _ _ THE BEACH PARTY.

In the word-wheels, find three party themes inspired by your adventures so far. Each word starts with the centre letter and uses all the letters in the wheel once.

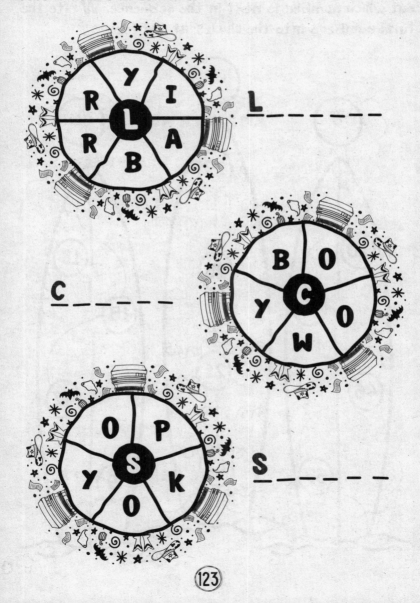

L _ _ _ _ _ _

C _ _ _ _ _ _

S _ _ _ _ _ _

Now you've helped Amanita, it's time to enjoy the beach party... for as long as possible!

Follow the numbers up each surf board and figure out which number is next in the sequence. Write the final numbers into the circles at the top.

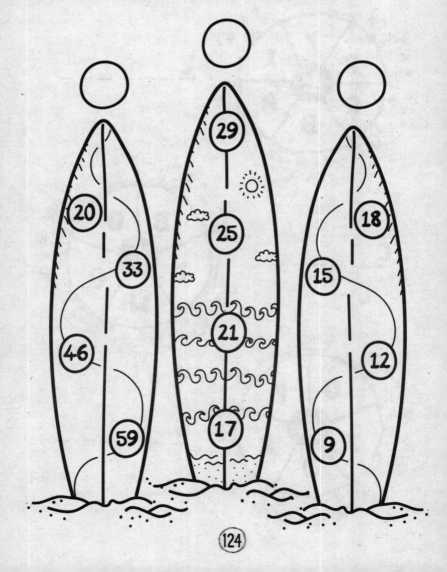

You and the pirate are slowly starting to disappear, but you still get time to have some party fun with the fairies: surfing, playing catch, eating shell cakes and drinking from a coconut!

Make your way from start to finish. You can move up, down or sideways but you can't move diagonally and you must follow the beach party items in this order:

CLUE LOGBOOK:
The Fairytale

In a moment, you will find out what happens next, now that you have helped to put the stories back together again...

But first, just take a minute to write down the last few clue letters you found in and around this fantasy fairytale land – you will need them!

Page : 107   Clue letter: ◯

Page : 109   Clue letter: ◯

Page : 111   Clue letter: ◯

Page : 115   Clue letter: ◯

Page : 122   Clue letter: ◯

The story continues...

This time, instead of disappearing then reappearing in another story, you leave the old book of stories completely...

Only, the book doesn't look old any more!

It is no longer tattered, and no more pages are falling apart. The book has a new charm and it is sparkling in the light.

You look up and realise that you are back in the big, colourful library.

Okbo looks very pleased with you...

Crack the code to finish the story!

Look back at all five Clue Logbooks on Pages 30, 54, 78, 102 and 126. Write the clue letters into the key below:

(For example, because you found the letter 'G' on Page 13, the letter 'G' is in the '13' box)

Once your key is complete, you can crack the code to reveal the story ending!

AS A R _ _ _ _ _ _ FOR YOUR
45 53 48 73 45 24

HELP PUTTING THE S _ _ _ _ _ B _ _ _ _
61 67 49 45 29   111 49 49 91

BACK TOGETHER, OKBO GIVES

YOU A B _ _ _, BLANK B _ _ _ _
111 70 13   111 49 49 91

"THIS B _ _ _ _ IS ENCHANTED,"
111 49 49 91

SAYS OKBO. "ANY S _ _ _ _ _ YOU
61 67 49 45 29

W _ _ _ _ _ IN ITS P _ _ _ _ _ WILL
48 45 70 67 53   16 73 13 53 61

COME TO L _ _ _ _, JUST LIKE THE
52 70 122 53

S _ _ _ _ _ W _ _ _ _ _ _ YOU EXPLORED.
61 67 49 45 29 48 49 45 52 24 61

YOU'RE ALWAYS WELCOME TO

R _ _ _ _ _ _ MY M _ _ _ _ _ _
45 53 93 70 61 70 67   62 73 13 70 43 73 52

L _ _ _ _ _ _ FOR I _ _ _ _ _ _ _ _ _ !"
52 70 111 45 73 45 29   70 21 61 16 70 45 73 67 70 49 21

WHAT S _ _ _ _ _ WILL YOU W _ _ _ _ _ ...?
61 67 49 45 29   48 45 70 67 53

Congratulations

You've completed your quest!
The adventure isn't over
just yet...

You'll find more Puzzle Quest fun
online at collins.co.uk/puzzlequest

But wait!

You'll need the secret password...

Use the key from page 128 to crack
the code and reveal your answer!

The secret password is

$\overline{73}$ $\overline{107}$ $\overline{67}$ $\overline{100}$ $\overline{49}$ $\overline{45}$

Puzzle

Answers

Page 10 – Tangled Paths

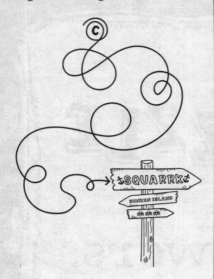

Page 12 – Wordsearch

Page 11 – Hide and Seek

Page 13 – Code-Cracker

MY SHIP CAME IN LATE AND I MISSED SQUARRK'S FOOD SHOPPING SEASON. NOW I HAVE ALL THIS FRESH FOOD AND NO ONE TO SELL IT TO. WOULD YOU LIKE TO BUY ANYTHING?

Page 14 – Follow the Path

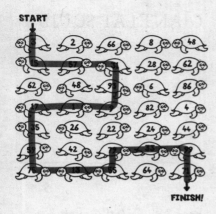

Page 15 – Silhouette Match

Page 16 – Word Scribble

AHOY!
DO YOU HAVE THE
PALM MAP?

Page 17 – Spot the Difference

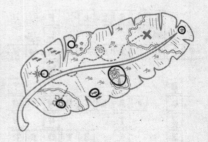

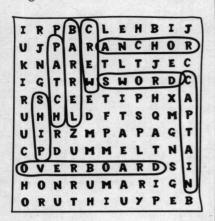

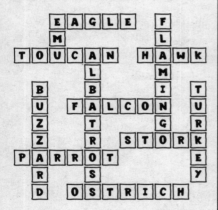

Page 22 – Code-Cracker

GIANT CAT SQUID

Page 23 – Code-Cracker

THE GIANT CAT SQUID
TRIES TO ATTACK THE
PIRATE SHIP, BUT YOU
USE YOUR BIG BALL OF
WOOL TO DISTRACT IT.
CATS LOVE PLAYING
WITH WOOL, BUT THIS
BIG SQUID'S TENTACLES
GOT ALL TANGLED UP,
GIVING YOU AND THE
CREW ENOUGH TIME
TO ESCAPE!

A – 5		O – 10	
B – 4		P – 7	
C – 15		Q – 8	
D – 12		R – 9	
E – 22		S – 33	
I – 6		T – 11	
L – 2		U – 14	
N – 3		W – 13	

Page 24 – Odd One Out

D is the odd one out

Page 25 – Wordfinder

BEARS

Page 26 – Sudoku

4	2	1	3
1	3	4	2
2	1	3	4
3	4	2	1

1	4	3	2
3	2	4	1
2	3	1	4
4	1	2	3

2	3	1	4
1	4	3	2
4	1	2	3
3	2	4	1

Page 27 – Maths Game

A 15 X 3 = 45

B 5 X 9 = 45

C 68 - 23 = 45

D 18 + 24 = 42

D is the odd one out

Page 28 – Sequence Puzzle

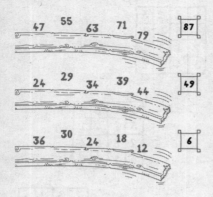

47 55 63 71 79 | 87

24 29 34 39 44 | 49

36 30 24 18 12 | 6

Page 29 – Code-Cracker

"GO BACK TO THE
MARKET IN
SQUARRK. FIND THE
SAD OTTER'S STALL.
THERE, YOU CAN GET
MORE THAN ENOUGH
FOOD FOR YOU AND
YOUR CREW
(YOU HAVE PLENTY
OF TREASURE NOW
TO PAY FOR IT!).
GOOD LUCK."

Pages 34 & 35 – Wordsearch

Page 36 – Spot the Difference

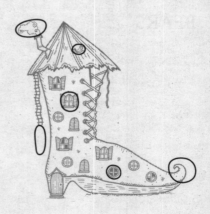

Page 37 – Sequence Puzzle

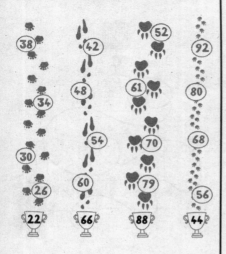

Page 38 – Letter Game

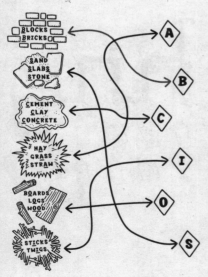

Page 39 – Maths Game

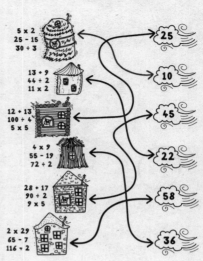

Page 40 – Maze

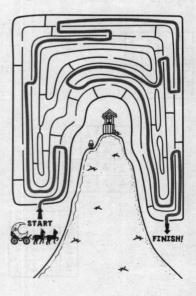

Page 41 – Missing Pieces

Page 43 – Tangled Paths

Page 42 – Sudoku

3	1	2	4
2	4	3	1
1	3	4	2
4	2	1	3

3	1	4	2
2	4	3	1
1	3	2	4
4	2	1	3

1	4	2	3
2	3	1	4
4	2	3	1
3	1	4	2

Page 44 – Order Game

Page 45 – Anagrams

SWEET PORRIDGE

PLAIN PORRIDGE

SPICY PORRIDGE

BAKED BEANS

Page 47 – Silhouette Match

1 — C

2 — A

3 — B

Page 46 – Silhouette Match

1 — B

2 — C

3 — A

Page 48 – Code-Cracker

SALOON STOOL

WAGON BED

Page 49 – Word-Wheels

PILLOW

SLIPPERS

MIRROR

Page 50 – Untangle

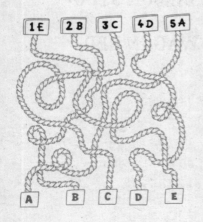

| 1E | 2B | 3C | 4D | 5A |

| A | B | C | D | E |

Page 51 – Follow the Path

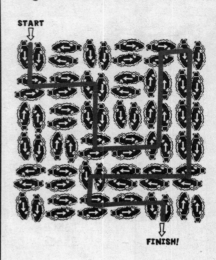

START

FINISH!

Page 52 – Word Scribble

COWABUNGA BILL

Page 53 – Code-Cracker

COWABUNGA BILL IS
NOT FROM THIS
STORY.
NOW THAT YOU HAVE
FOUND THIS COWBOY
COW, YOU BOTH START
TO DISAPPEAR. SAY
"BYE" TO THE BEARS!

A – 9	O – 14
B – 15	P – 4
D – 24	R – 12
E – 30	S – 8
G – 18	T – 22
I – 7	U – 6
L – 5	W – 20
N – 2	Y – 3

Page 59 – Silhouette Match

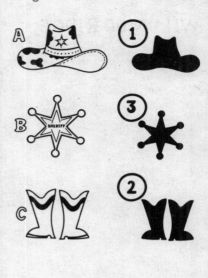

Page 58 – Spot the Difference

Pages 60 & 61 – Kriss Kross

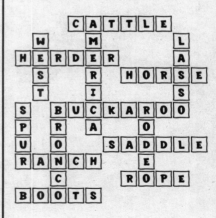

Page 62 – Code-Cracker

WILDMOO RIDGE

Pages 64 & 65 – Wordsearch

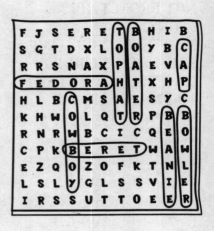

Page 63 – Spot the Difference

Page 66 – Word-Wheels

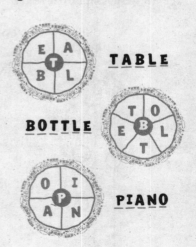

TABLE

BOTTLE

PIANO

POSTER

1. EATEN MOST OF THE BEAN CROPS IN WILDMOO RIDGE!

2. SCARED ALL THE CUSTOMERS AWAY FROM THE SALOON.

3. SCARED ALL THE MINER COWS AWAY FROM THE GOLD MINES.

4. RUINED THE WATER BY GETTING SLIME IN THE WILDMOO WELL!

C is the odd one out

Page 71 – Maze

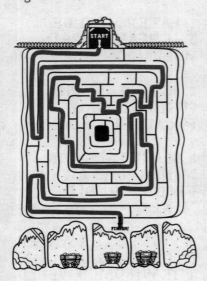

Page 72 – Order Game

Pages 73 – Code-Cracker

YOU SET A TRAP THEN
WATCH AND WAIT,
THE MONSTER EATS
BEANS YOU SET AS BAIT.
YOU PULL THE LEVER AT
THE RIGHT TIME,
DOWN COMES A CAGE TO
TRAP THE SLIME.
THE MONSTER IS CAUGHT
WITHIN THE CART,
SO YOU AND THE SHERIFF
JUMP IN AND DEPART.

A – 3	M – 11
B – 2	N – 6
C – 25	P – 24
E – 5	R – 8
G – 12	S – 1
H – 40	T – 10
I – 7	U – 14
L – 9	W – 16

Page 74 – Sequence Puzzle

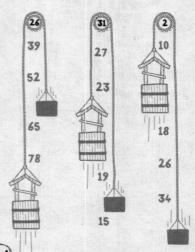

26
39
52
65
78

31
27
23
19
15

2
10
18
26
34

Page 75 – Follow the Path

Page 77 – Word Scribble

YOU ARE MADE
DEPUTY SHERIFF
OF THE TOWN
AND GIVEN A
SHINY BADGE!

Page 76 – Sudoku

4	2	3	1
3	1	4	2
2	3	1	4
1	4	2	3

3	1	4	2
4	2	3	1
2	4	1	3
1	3	2	4

4	3	2	1
1	2	3	4
3	4	1	2
2	1	4	3

Pages 82 & 83 – Wordsearch

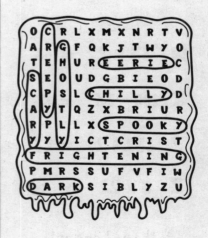

Page 84 – Unscramble

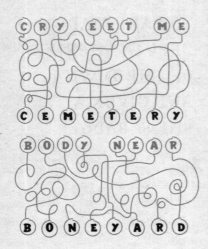

CRY EET ME

CEMETERY

BODY NEAR

BONEYARD

Page 85 – Maths Game

W $33 \times 2 = 66$

X $100 - 36 = 64$

Y $132 \div 2 = 66$

Z $3 \times 22 = 66$

X is the odd one out

Page 86 – Sequence Puzzle

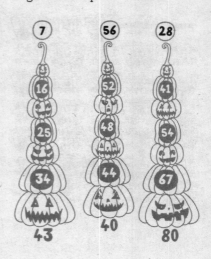

Page 87 – Wordsearch

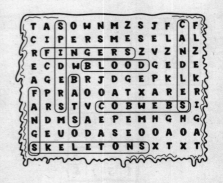

Page 88 – Letter Game

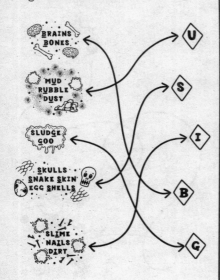

Pages 90 & 91 – Kriss Kross

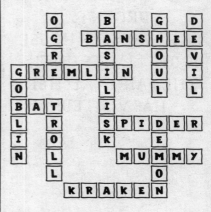

Page 89 – Odd One Out

C is the odd one out

Page 92 – Spot the Difference

Page 93 – Word Scribble

URGENT!
THE HAUNTED HOUSE
IS OFF LIMITS UNTIL
THE FAIRY-CATCHER
HAS VISITED!

Page 95 – Tangled Paths

Page 94 – Sudoku

3	2	1	4
4	1	2	3
2	3	4	1
1	4	3	2

4	3	2	1
2	1	4	3
1	2	3	4
3	4	1	2

1	3	4	2
4	2	1	3
2	4	3	1
3	1	2	4

Page 96 – Maze

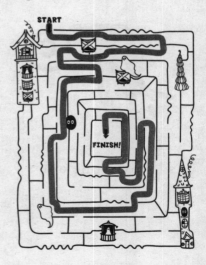

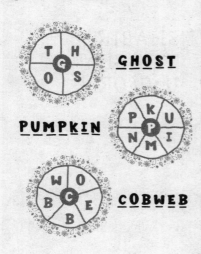

GHOST

PUMPKIN

COBWEB

THE BLACK CATS
ARE BRIGHT GREEN!
THE SKELETONS
ARE DANCING!
THE CHANDELIER IS
NOW A DISCO BALL!
THE BATS HAVE
BUTTERFLY WINGS!

A – 12	K – 4
C – 3	L – 5
E – 16	N – 6
F – 8	O – 22
G – 10	R – 7
H – 27	T – 11
I – 9	U – 14

START

FINISH!

I DIDN'T MEAN TO
SCARE ALL THE
CREATURES AWAY!
I SUDDENLY
ARRIVED IN
THIS SPOOKY PLACE
AND I WAS JUST TRY-
ING TO MAKE
IT FEEL MORE COSY!
CAN YOU TAKE ME
HOME?

Page 101 – Follow the Path

Page 107 – Word Scribble

SHABIRA
THE SHY
UNICORN

Page 106 – Wordfinder

Page 108 – Sequence Puzzle

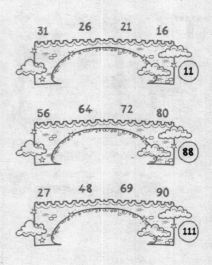

Page 109 – Tangled Paths

Page 112 – Spot the Difference

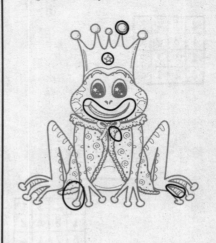

Pages 110 & 111 – Kriss Kross

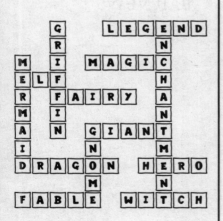

Page 113 – Follow the Path

Page 114 – Suduko

2	1	4	3
4	3	2	1
1	4	3	2
3	2	1	4

1	3	2	4
4	2	3	1
3	4	1	2
2	1	4	3

2	4	3	1
1	3	4	2
3	2	1	4
4	1	2	3

Pages 116 & 117 – Wordsearch

Page 115 – Odd One Out

Z is the odd one out

Page 118 – Code-Cracker

BAD NEWS

Page 119 – Code-Cracker

SORRY AMANITA.
WHILE YOU WERE
GONE SOMEONE NEW
CAME ALONG WITH
LOTS OF FUN PARTY
IDEAS. WE HIRED
THEM AS THE NEW
HEAD OF THE CLUB.
BUT YOU CAN GET
YOUR JOB BACK IF YOU
THINK OF SOME NEW
PARTY THEMES THAT
ARE FUN AND FRESH!

A – 19   N – 15
B – 5   O – 6
D – 24   R – 3
E – 11   S – 16
F – 14   T – 10
H – 36   W – 12
I – 9   Y – 13

Page 120 – Silhouette Match

Page 121 – Maze

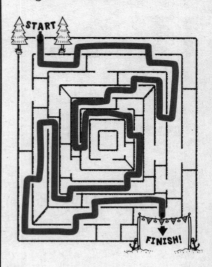

Page 122 – Code-Craker

YOU TELL AMANITA
ABOUT YOUR
ADVENTURES AND
HELP THEM PLAN
SOME PARTIES
INSPIRED BY YOUR
TRAVELS THROUGH
STORIES.

THE IDEAS ARE SO
FUN AND FRESH
THAT THE FAIRIES
AGREE AMANITA CAN
BE HEAD OF PARTY
PLANNING AGAIN
AFTER THE BEACH

Page 123 – Word-Wheels

LIBRARY

COWBOY

SPOOKY

Page 125 – Order Game

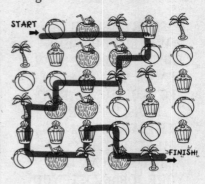

START

FINISH!

Page 124 – Sequence Puzzle

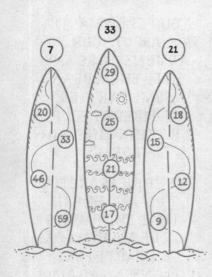

7

33

21

Page 128 – Clue Code

G	P	N	D	Y
13	16	21	24	29

C	R	W	O	L	E
43	45	48	49	52	53

S	M	T	I	A
61	62	67	70	73

X	K	V	Q	H
85	91	93	95	100

U	J	B	Z	F
107	109	111	115	122

AS A REWARD FOR YOUR HELP PUTTING THE STORY BOOK BACK TOGETHER, OKBO GIVES YOU A BIG, BLANK BOOK.

"THIS BOOK IS ENCHANTED," SAYS OKBO. "ANY STORY YOU WRITE IN ITS PAGES WILL COME TO LIFE, JUST LIKE THE STORY WORLDS YOU EXPLORED. YOU'RE ALWAYS WELCOME TO REVISIT MY MAGICAL LIBRARY FOR INSPIRATION!" WHAT STORY WILL YOU WRITE...?

NOTES

(Blank 'notes' pages like this are handy
for jotting down any notes or working
out when you're busy solving puzzles!

You could also use them
to write, doodle or
anything else you'd
like to do while
on your quest!)

NOTES

NOTES